Prayers

of

Prophetic

Declaration

Yvonne Martinez

D1110300

Prayers of Prophetic Declaration

Reprint Copyright @ 2013 by Yvonne Martinez
Copyright © 2010 by Yvonne Martinez
All rights reserved

This book is protected by the copyright law of the United States of
America. This book may not be copied or reprinted for commercial gain
or profit. The use of short quotations or occasional page copying
for personal or group study is
permitted and encouraged.
Permission will be granted upon request.

Unless otherwise noted, all Scripture quotations are from
the Holy Bible,
New International Version. Copyright © 1973, 1978, 1984,
International Bible Society. Used by permission of Zondervan.
All rights reserved.

The "NIV" and "New International Version" trademarks are
registered in the United States Patent and Trademark Office by
International Bible Society.
Use of either trademark requires the permission of
International Bible Society.

ISBN 1450582435

EAN 13 9781450582438.

Printed in the United States of America

**Distributed by
yvonnem.org**

Dedication

To my precious friend,
Lydia McChesney, the gift of your
beautiful presence is deeply missed.

I honor you with the writing of these
prophetic prayers as a reminder
our legacy of faith in God prevails.

4

Introduction

You will decree a thing and it will be established for you and light will shine on your ways (Job 22:28 NASB).

Words satisfy the mind as much as fruit does the stomach; good talk is as gratifying as a good harvest. Words kill, words give life; they're either poison or fruit—you choose (Proverbs 18:20-22 Message Bible).

Nothing happens in the Kingdom without first a declaration is made. In Genesis, God declared and formed our world with His Words. When God spoke He demonstrated the power of prophetic declaration. Prophetic declaration was God's first creative act!

We pray with declaration to exercise our authority as Jesus commissioned. Our declarations unlock Heaven and Heaven's power is released.

From the place of rest and faith in the accomplished work of Jesus' death, blood and resurrection, *Prayers of Prophetic Declaration* partners with God's Word to release His Kingdom on earth as it is in Heaven!

It is time to quit asking our Heavenly Father to do something He has already done in Christ and given us authority to replicate. It is time to decree, proclaim, and declare the things He has already completed through Jesus.

Prayers of Prophetic Declaration will shift the atmosphere to receive His provision and purpose for you.

- Issue legislation with authority given to us by God, Himself.
- Announce God's word has preeminence over what we see in the natural and demand it acquiesce to the spoken, living Word.
- Release Heaven on earth.

Grow into the person He as called you to be by coming into agreement with His Word.

Table of Contents

Table of Contents

-continued-

-1-

Favor

"For he says, "In the time of my favor I heard you, and in the day of salvation I helped you. I tell you, now is the time of God's favor, now is the day of salvation." 2Cor 6:2

You knew me before the foundations of the earth. I walk in a deeper revelation of the goodness You speak over me because I am Your workmanship in Christ Jesus.

I receive the visions of Your heart for me. My destiny is secure.

I walk in the Spirit and not after the flesh, enabling me to bring forth one hundred-fold fruit. I bring You Glory in all I do and say.

I cooperate with You to bring Your Glory to all men. My whole heart is surrendered for Your service. You created me with the ability to multiply. I choose to multiply goodness and truth to glorify You in my life.

Faith arises with wings of hope and expectation and I mount up and fly into the promises, into the purposes You have for me. You are, indeed, multiplying me in every way.

Father God, it is an awesome thought to know You not only created Heaven and earth for my habitation, but You created me as an exquisite habitation for You and a temple to house Your glorious Presence.

You have given me the gift of free will. You allow me to choose to respond to Your call and Your loving embrace. I am motivated to react in positive ways, taking all You have promised at face value. I believe and I receive.

I walk in complete freedom and not in performance. I choose to walk in a manner which demonstrates You are worth living for.

I choose to enter into a renewed covenant with You today, knowing You rescued me from darkness and placed me into the Kingdom of Your Son.

I look upon You and Your awesome beauty. How wonderful and mighty You are.

There is no condemnation for those who are in Christ Jesus for You triumph over the law of sin and death. I cannot be loved any more than I am right now. No more performance, for it is by the Cross of Your Son, Jesus, I am saved.

I am free to be me, your designed creation, created like no other. Favor, blessing, and every good thing is mine as I dwell in You.

-2-

Love

"In this way, love is made complete among us so that we will have confidence…" 1John 4:17

I receive the sweet taste of Your Word. It settles around my heart and flows into the hidden places of dryness like fresh spring water. It coats my heart like thick honey from the Rock. My eyes behold You. I see into the realms of Your glory reserved for me in this day. My heart responds to You.

Your eyes are fixed on me and my eyes are fixed upon You. You are Love, therefore I lock my heart with Yours in one accord. We walk together in the intimate secret place of our love.

I see all the beauty of who You are and how You made me.

Your kindness flows to me from the depths of Your heart. The gates of purpose and destiny are swinging wide open.

All that has been stolen is being returned and multiplied unto me. Spring is here.

Your Presence softens the soil of my heart. I am being made new. Flowers of provision in every area of my life are popping up just as I need them. Spring is here.

I envelope myself within the comfort of Your Presence and love is awakening within me. Your very life flows through the veins of my being and I am being made like You. The very essence of who You made me to be is awakening like the rising of the dawn. This is a new day, and I embrace it.

I hand You all my excuses. I lay aside every hindrance and receive restoration of all things stolen from me. I receive divine appointments and circumstances without inadequacy or doubt.

Old things have passed away and Heavenly waterfalls are prepared to drink from. I come into Your Presence and I drink deeply.

I express You in unique and beautiful ways. The best part of my life is now. I am free. I open my wings to fly with You.

16

-3-

Dream

"In the last days, God says, I will pour out my Spirit on all people. Your sons and daughters will prophesy, your young men will see visions, your old men will dream dreams."
Acts 2:17

Lord, there are many dreams deposited by You. My heart rejoices. Lord, You are my dream maker; my dream fulfilled in every way. There is none like You.

I am of good courage and I live the dreams You have for me. I receive the understanding that I am with You as You are with me to fulfill the visions You place in my heart. I am thankful no one or nothing can stop what You put into motion to fulfill my destiny. I worship You and praise You through the intimacy we have together.

It is in an atmosphere of worshipping You where I receive all the dreams and visions You have for me to receive. I desire only the destiny and purpose You have created me to walk in. Let it unfold and be manifested in my life now and for all eternity.

Lord, what an honor to be Your temple - to be Your plan for spreading the dreams and provisions of Your heart. I thank You and praise You forever for Your love is indescribable and endures to the very end. I will worship You day and night as I praise You with my whole heart. My greatest desire is for deeper, intimate communion, and intimacy with You so I may live out your plans.

Yes, Lord, I am Your dwelling place, a habitation for Your glory. I am filled with Your Presence. I am a part of Your plan. You trust me with the thoughts and intents of Your heart to be Your dream come true. Praise You for opportunities to participate in the sprinkling of Your glory in the earth.

You care about all the dreams You have given me. You have not forgot the promises and covenants you made with me. You make way for their fulfillment. I'll praise You for eternity as I receive the revelation that I am Your dream come true. I am a manifest dream of Your heart. It is all too wonderful to comprehend.

I am ready and willing to be poured out among the people so Your dreams, visions and passion may be revealed among men. I am in agreement with You, Lord, and acknowledge I have been made righteous through Your Blood to be a vessel of honor hosting Your Presence.

You take pleasure in me. I declare the work You started in me shall be completed and bring glory to Your name. I stretch my tent pegs in order to dream bigger, for I am a co-laborer with You to carry out Your mission in the earth.

It is Your promptings in my spirit which move me and motivate me to live and dream big. I declare that I am obedient to all You desire to do with me and through me. As I acknowledge You in all my ways, You direct my steps to accomplish that which You have planted into my heart.

You ignite the passions of my heart to fulfill Your will in the earth. All my dreams originate with You and will come to pass as I come into agreement with Your Word to me.

You take my dreams to a new level as I surrender my imagination and reach out and take ahold of Your hand in this adventure.

Dreams, given by You and inspired by You, become reality.

-4-

Faith

"For the word of the Lord is right and true; he is faithful in all he does." Psalm 33:4

You are the love of My life and the truth that sets me free. I set my affections on things above and choose not to believe circumstance has the power to determine the outcome of my life. I look to You, the author and finisher of my faith, not anything or anyone else. I do not allow the enemy of my soul to cause me to focus my attention on myself, my past failures, or the lies of the enemy.

My focus is on You Lord. I choose to not be distracted by my own agendas or allow myself to become overburdened with activities that are substitutes for relationship with You.

I close my eyes to the distractions around me. I praise You as I receive help from on high. I come and rest in the all-sufficiency of Your name and in Your Word. It is not by might or by power but by Your Spirit that all things are accomplished. Therefore, I come into rest - into oneness with your Spirit.

I am changing and growing daily in Your revelation and understanding. My heart is being transformed into the likeness of the Lord in all I do and say. I dwell in the overshadowing Presence of the Lord at all times. He is my covering. My soul is being sanctified daily as I submit myself to the Lord. I am in Him and He is in me now.

Lord, You are the Light of the world and the Light of my heart. You never shift or change. There is no shadow of turning in You; therefore, *when You came to dwell in me, the complete Light of Your Presence came without variation.*

You are constant and steady. You do not faint or grow weary and Your help is ever-present and ready. My help comes from You. No setback, no hindrance or problem can separate me from the finished, revelatory work of the Cross.

You never cease releasing Your ever-flowing fountain of grace and mercy. How wonderful You are. There is none like You. I position myself to receive from the river of Your heart and all it provides. It is Your help continually flowing into my life every moment which sustains me. As a tree planted by the river, my leaves will never dry. You are my ever-present help, flowing deeply within my spirit, drawing me toward you.

I am born again. I am a child of the Father. You are attentive to the sound of my voice. Not only are You always near to me, You are in me – Christ, the hope of all glory.

As I draw near to You in my thoughts and actions, You draw near to me in visible and manifest ways. My heart responds to the movement of Your Spirit.

Papa God, You have sent ministering angels on my behalf. As we walk together, I abide in You. The work of the Cross is finished and the resurrection life of Christ is in me, for I am an overcomer. Together we light up the darkness.

My heart is open to the nearness of the Lord and is attentive to the sound of His voice. I have drawn near to the Lord and He has drawn near to me. He is here now.

-5-

Shield

"You give me your shield of victory, and your right hand sustains me; you stoop down to make me great."
Psalm 18:35

I declare and proclaim this day that I am strong in the Lord and the power of His might. I have on the full armor of God and I stand against schemes conspired against me. The battle was won and I have victory in Christ, Jesus.

In all ways I stand in courage, victorious in You. I come into agreement with Your Word and say I am healed, delivered and serving You, Lord, with all my might.

I gird my loins with the truth so all lies must flee from this place of power. This is my spiritual authority. I am now filled with the light of the Truth which causes darkness to flee.

I put the breastplate of righteousness over the deepest core of my being, so my emotions are kind, patient, merciful and compassionate. I receive the great love You have for me. Your great love flows through my spirit. Thank You, Jesus, for Your Blood which covers me and makes me righteous.

I wash the dust of the past off my feet with the gospel of peace. All fears from my childhood and adulthood must now flee for I walk in peace and contentment in You, Papa.

Your peace dispels anger, resentment and frustration. Your peace, which passes all understanding, is now made manifest in my heart and mind.

Above all I take up the shield of faith and hold it in front of my heart so that every fiery dart of the enemy must be quenched.

I put the helmet of salvation on my head and declare I have the mind of Christ which is all right thinking and action. Papa God did not give me a spirit of fear but He has given me a spirit of power, love and a sound mind. My mind and soul are at peace.

I take up the sword of the spirit and hold it over body, my innermost being and declare old things have passed away and all things have become new. The old man of my flesh is dead and the new man of the spirit lives.

I speak to mistrust, unforgiveness, anger, disappointment, fear and self-protection. I say, "I renounce any agreement with you, be removed and cast into the sea!"

I thank You Lord that I am forgiven and I love You with all my heart, all my soul, and my entire mind. I hunger and thirst for righteousness and I have found it in You.

Deeper faith awakens and stirs a hunger and thirst for more of You.

Thank You for who You are in my life: Father, Son and Holy Spirit. Only You, Lord, are worthy of all honor, glory and praise.

-6-

Dance

"Then maidens will dance and be glad, young men and old as well…" Jer. 31:13

Release Your resurrection power and dance over me and I shall live to fulfill all that has ever been planned for me.

I arise and I worship!
I arise and I proclaim!
I arise and dance the dance of victory!

This day, I choose to look to You and Your resurrection power and might on my behalf. You are committed to seeing me obtain every victory and gave the ultimate sacrifice to do so.

29

I do all things by Your Spirit. By grace and with faith I come into agreement with Your Word. You are sufficient in my weakness. I can do all things through You who strengthens me.

I am an overcomer and You have put me on the right course. You are my Resurrection Life and nothing is impossible with You. One breath of Your Spirit and everything is made new.

You are good and You reward those who seek You and believe in Your name. I believe in You.

Papa God, I rise and shine with a heart of joy for You are faithful. Your love endures forever. I acknowledge Your loving-kindness and Your complete attention to even my smallest concern.

I hear the whispers of Your voice over the rattling of dry bones. Faith will hear me speak Your Word and faith will come. The ears of faith are open to the Word coming out of my mouth. Resurrection life is today.

You create in me a clean heart and a steadfast spirit. I choose to arise and worship You with a heart of faith. I receive the ability to move and the ability to dance. The framework of my life is being built line upon line, tissue upon tissue and muscle upon muscle. Dry bones are resurrected to bring forth life.

I declare that I am becoming more responsive to Your movement, moment by moment. Every nerve and fiber of my being is coming into alignment with You.

I dance in my heart. I dance with my feet. I will dance regardless of what I see, feel or think. I am moving in motion to the beating of Your heart...to the inhaling and exhaling of Your very breath. I am in perfect step with Your lead.

I mount up with the wings of an eagle and I soar to the heights of promise.

I arise and I worship!
I arise and I proclaim!
I arise and dance the dance of victory!

Prayers of Prophetic Declaration

-7-

Life

"For just as the Father raises the dead and gives them life,
even so the Son gives life to whom he is pleased to give it."
John 5:21

Father, my eyes see the fullness, wonder and power of You, a Living Word revealing the source and essence of life.

I take my thoughts captive and walk according to the Spirit. I am wise as a serpent and gentle as a dove.

I feel my heart softening, becoming tender in response to You and the Words You have spoken to me. I am slow to anger and quick to repent, and my heart is alive with Your redemption.

I receive Your Word as a Living Word. Every syllable of Your Word implanted within my heart will not return void. It will accomplish and bring about Your purposes within me and around me.

I choose to agree with You Father. I choose to agree with the Word. I will meditate, think on and come into vocal agreement with all You have said to me. Today I draw near to You and You draw near to me.

My thinking is transformed by ingesting Your Word. I live not according to natural bread but every Word that proceeds from Your mouth.

Your Word is life. Your Spirit is life. Your Presence is ever increasing my capacity to live in abundance. You are life and because You are alive in me, I live in cohabitation with Your Presence. Your Kingdom is today. I come into agreement with You and I live.

-8-

Freedom

"Now the Lord is the Spirit, and where the Spirit of the Lord is, there is freedom." 2Cor 3:17

Lord, You are my strength and my song. Your name is above all other names and I run into Your strong tower where I am safe from my enemies. You spread Yourself over me like the heavens cover the earth. I am enclosed within Your canopy of love and protection. Your goodness surrounds me like a thick blanket.

You stir the creative gifts placed within me that I might represent a visible picture of You to all I meet. I believe, receive and embrace You.

I am seated with You in heavenly places positioned to hear and see what You are doing in every situation. By faith I am one who rules and reigns with You. Every thought contrary to the Word is cast down.

Your Presence surrounds me and covers me with such a splendid love. You provide all I need to be sustained physically, emotionally, and spiritually. My life and heart are in Your hands. I run into the strong tower of Your might and strength where I am saved from my enemies. My heart is a deep well of realized love and grace.

I rise up in the calling You have placed on my life and I will not be dismayed by the unkind Words of men. You are mighty to save and have set me in a large place where I can move with freedom and grace. Everything in my life is turned for good and the plans of my enemy do not prosper.

I proclaim Your name. I guard my heart and mouth that I may speak what is lovely and upright at all times.

Lord, I receive a new day. I receive a new heart in everything I do. It is for freedom that You set me free. I do not entangle myself with the cares of the world or with bondage of the past.

Your grace covers me and upholds me. Mercy surrounds me like a cloak. My hands are made to declare Your works and they shall do so continually.

My family is standing under the covering of Your redemptive love and grace. My family is loved beyond measure and each member will come into their destiny according to Your plan and purpose. I rest in Your all-sufficient grace, Papa God.

Today is a new day and I embrace complete freedom. I rejoice in You and I am glad.

-9-

Heart

"Above all else, guard your heart, for it is the wellspring of life." Proverbs 4:23

I am after the Lord's heart and the Word planted in me is now pushing roots downward and growing fruit upward. I am an oak of righteousness planted by streams of Living Water and I bring forth good fruit. Everything I do shall prosper as my soul prospers.

You are my light and my shield, an every present help in time of trouble, therefore each step I take is ordered by You. Every rough place is made smooth and every uneven place is made into a plain. I do not falter and I stand upright in a large place meant just for me. My heart trusts in the Lord. The goodness and mercy of the Lord follow me in all I do and in all I am a part of.

The love of the Lord is set upon me and I am in His fixed gaze. My face is set like flint and I shall not be confused. My heart rejoices that help comes from Papa God."

Yes, the Lord is my light and my salvation. I have no one to fear. The light of the Lord is illumining my heart and is ever present with me. I will never be forgotten or left alone.

My path is being bathed in light, revelation, Wisdom, understanding and a deep and intimate knowledge the Lord's plan for me. I walk uprightly with a heart of faith and do not waver with the shifting winds of doubt and unbelief. I have the mind of Christ and contain the thoughts and intents of the Lord's heart.

I hear the Shepherd's voice and I do not follow another.

Every promise given to me is yes and amen. I have love, power and a sound mind and discern the timing and purposes of the Lord.

I am not missing one plan or purpose You have for me. The eyes of my heart are opened. I gird myself with the Word and the promises You have made to me and press on to my high calling in You.

I abide in the green pastures and still waters of You. I live in the righteousness, joy and peace of the Holy Spirit.

My head rests on Your chest and I hear Your heart beat. I align my heart to pattern Yours and I am at rest.

-10-

Lion

"...and he gave a loud shout like the roar of a lion. When he shouted, the voices of the seven thunders spoke."
Rev 10:3

Lord, I glorify You for You are worthy to open the book. You are the great Lion of the tribe of Judah. Thank You for inviting me to ride with You. I desire to abandon all I have trusted in and cling to You. In You alone am I safe.

I walk consistently in discernment as I spend time with You. I am protected from those who would seek to hurt me. You are my Deliverer, my Rock, and my Fortress. You rescued me from the kingdom of darkness and brought me into the Kingdom of Light.

I praise You for all eternity with a thankful heart. I bury my face in the mane of Your Presence, fearing no one or anything for You are with me. You never leave me nor forsake me. I come to ride with You, singing songs of thanksgiving and deliverance.

Roar over my life. My heart is purified. I am Your workmanship. I trust in the complete work You are doing in me. I give You all thanks for that which You alone can do, for I know that without You I can do nothing. I come to You with a thankful heart. I praise You for the reality of all You are.

I acknowledge You in all I do, and You establish my thoughts. Godliness with contentment is great gain and I have great gain in You.

Lord, I count it all joy for I know You never leave me or forsake me. I am content in the midst of trials and tribulations yoked with faith that You are with me. I fear no evil.

You teach me to follow Your ways, cloud by day or fire by night. I follow where You lead and my discernment is increased. I have wisdom to know how to deal with all that You reveal to me. I let patience have its perfect work in me, praising You in the midst of the trying of my faith, knowing I lack nothing.

Father, I have eyes to see all that I need to see. I adjust my focus to watch and I adjust my ears to hear. I learn timing and patience is of utmost importance. I listen and wait on Your leading to proceed. I rest in your perfect timing. Rest is actionable and alert to everything around it I abide in You.

You, Lord, are my Savior, my Lion of Judah, always guarding over me. You are my refuge and my strength. In Your Presence I am safe.

Prayers of Prophetic Declaration

-11-

Trust

"Trust in the Lord with all your heart and lean not on your own understanding." Proverbs 3:5

I walk in a place of quiet confidence for You have given me peace and my mind is not troubled or afraid. Your angels are watching over me, therefore, no evil or plague comes near me. My mind is stayed on You and I do not have a spirit of fear. The love planted in my heart evicts all fear. I walk in love, power and a sound mind.

Like a good shepherd watching over his sheep, You are watching over me. Your rod and staff comfort me.

I do not have a spirit of bondage to fear for I am adopted into Your family and You are my "Abba Father". You are my helper and no man has power over me.

I dwell in the secret place, under the shadow of Your wings. I abide in You and You alone, covered by Your Presence. I do not put my trust in men, nor am I afraid of the terrors of night or the arrows flying by day. I am wearing the armor of Papa God which extinguishes the fiery darts of the enemy. Truth girds my loins. I hold the thoughts and the intents of the Lord.

I am established in righteousness by the Blood of Christ. You hear my every Word and Your hands are stretched out to me. The goodness of God, laid up for me in Christ Jesus, is manifesting in Me and I am in perfect peace. Your light, life and salvation are perfected in me.

No weapon formed against me can prosper and all tongues raised up against me are judged by the Lord. I am protected under the shadow of your wings.

My heart is in perfect peace for all my thoughts are on You. My heart meditates on You day and night and I trust in You.

Every day of my life is established in peace and fear is far from me.

Prayers of Prophetic Declaration

50

-12-

Understand

"Then he opened their minds so they could understand the Scriptures." Luke 24:45

You have called me by my name and I answer your call, seeking You at every opportunity. The eyes of my heart are open to see You in the fullness of Your glory. The windows of Heaven are opened to pour out wisdom and revelation into my daily life. You have given me insight into the great mysteries of Your Word that I might walk in understanding and truth.

I desire intimate knowledge of You—to see Your face. Your are flooding my spirit with light and revelation that I can know and understand all You reveal to me; that I might know and understand the true richness of all I have inherited in You.

I have been set-apart for You. You flood my heart with light and I understand the hope You have called me to. Nothing separates me from Your immeasurable and unlimited love. This is the love I walk in, live in, and breathe in.

I am seated in heavenly places with You and You are seated far above all powers and dominions. You have been seated above every name and title. I belong to Papa God by the precious Blood of sacrifice Jesus gave and I partake of His resurrection power—a power able to raise me from the dead while I am yet living. Therefore I have access to Heaven's Throne, receiving truth and revelation.

As I walk in this understanding my eyes and heart will have true and clear vision which the world cannot corrupt or dissuade. My heart is open to understand and have revelation of the *greatness of Your power in me—the same power that raised You from the dead. This same power lives within me and I am seated in heavenly places with You. I come out of agreement with restriction and religious form and I rise up in Your authority, power and dominion.*

The eyes of my heart are opened enabling me to walk as You walked, commune with the Father as You did, and to do the works You did. I am a seeker of You and You apprehend me to fill me overflowing with wisdom and understanding.

Prayers of Prophetic Declaration

-13-

Provision

"So Abraham called that place, 'The Lord Will Provide'. And to this day it is said, "On the mountain of the Lord it will be provided." Gen 22:14

I am loved by my Father God with abundance because I am His child. My heart is fully open to obtain all He has for me. I receive the gracious gift of His heart today for He is a perfect Father in every way. All good gifts come from His hand and His hand is stretched out to me, full and running over.

He provides for me in every area of my life. Everything I need is found in His giving heart. Not one moment of my life escapes His attention and in the process He infuses me with hope for He loves me with an everlasting love.

The thoughts of the Lord toward me cannot be counted and are as numerous as the sands of the seashore. He rejoices over me with singing and is doing good toward me for I am His treasured possession. I am established by the Father for the complete desire of His heart.

Nothing is impossible with Papa God. He establishes my purpose and my destiny is His priority. He shows me great and mighty things and I will not miss His plans for me. I do not follow another or the voice of my own negative thinking or self-talk.

I seek the Lord with my whole heart. My heart belongs to the Lord and the Lord alone. I am a seeker and a finder of the Lord. The delight of my heart is in and for the Lord alone. I am delighting in Him and am receiving the desires of His heart as my own.

Nothing is impossible and He is doing more than I could ever imagine with my life through *the power of love and constant encouragement. The Lord is my encourager today and I depend on Him and do not sway to any negative words of men. I am comforted by His Truth, which is without waiver or change.*

I am a fortified city, a light on the hill and nothing can by any means harm me as I abide in the secret place of His love. The Lord is close to me in my brokenness and loves me with a tender heart, calling me His own. Offenses have no power over me for I give all broken heartedness to Him and leave no room for judgment or unforgiveness. I surrender every broken or offended place to Him as He carries me like a shepherd carries his sheep.

The Lord God is my Father, a Papa like no other and I am His child. I am loved by the Father as much as Jesus is loved by Him. As I abide in Jesus and Jesus abides in me the love of the Father is revealed in my life through His shed Blood on the Cross.

When I see Jesus I see the Father and when I know Jesus I know the Father, for He is an exact representation of the Father.

The demonstration of the Father's love is manifest in Jesus and because Jesus is in me I also am a representation of the Father's love as I walk according to the leading and guiding of the Holy Spirit.

-14-

Health

"Jesus said to him, "I will go and heal him." Matt 8:7

I am washed white as snow and my sins are not counted against me. The blood of Jesus represents the true love of Papa God for me I receive all His Blood has done for me. I am loved and I love. I have life abundant.

Jesus bore my grief and sorrows and took the punishment of my sin and gave me life eternal. The Cross was full payment for my iniquities and therefore, Papa God pours all His healing goodness into me.

Papa God listens to me whenever I ask or need anything and He answers from the loving kindness of His heart.

The Spirit of the sovereign Lord is upon me to heal the broken hearted and set the captives free. The blind will see and the lame will walk. The prisoners are released and captives are set free.

Jesus gave me the keys to the Kingdom. I take the key to healing and claim my full inheritance in the Kingdom. His Kingdom is manifest in me.

I am in Jesus and Jesus is in the Father. I have been given authority to heal the sick, cast out demons and cleanse lepers. I partner with Jesus to heal every kind of sickness and disease, infirmity and trauma.

-15-

Royalty

"But you are a chosen people, a royal priesthood, a holy nation, a people belonging to God, that you may declare the praises of him who called you out of darkness into his wonderful light." 1Peter 2:9

According to Your Word, Lord Jesus, I am a king and priest, washed by Your Blood. My heart is a heart of flesh, soft and pliable, held within the palm of Your hand. You have cupped Yourself around me and have become my rear guard. I have taken captive all my thoughts and my meditations are on You. I think on what is lovely, upright and true, letting no unwholesome word come out of my mouth.

My mouth is anointed with kindness and its words supply grace and edification to the hearer.

I live, I move, and have my being in You because my face is set like flint toward the mountain where my help comes from. I am no longer of this earth for I am seated in heavenly places with an ear to hear the conversations of heaven. The eyes of my spirit are opened.

My gates have given You entrance, and my mouth flows from a sweet fountain. I draw deeply from the wells of salvation, taking every portion of healing and deliverance it offers.

My thoughts are not on the things of this world for You have captivated my heart. My soul is consumed by You.

I delight in Your Word and I obey Your commands. You have manifested Yourself to me in plain sight that I might not miss Your face. My steps have been directed by You before the beginning of time. I have always been in Your heart and now I am formed into an intricate *piece of Your DNA. I am infused with your creative power.*

My heart is in Your hand and I am wholly surrendered for I love obedience better than sacrifice. I am Your temple, Your dwelling place. I am in You and You are in me. I am captivated for You have captured my heart. I am apprehended for you have apprehended my spirit.

Graces upon graces embrace me. Mercies upon mercies encompass me. Love upon love infuses me. Forgiveness upon forgiveness emanates from me. Wisdom upon wisdom is dispensed unto me. Your fullness dwells within me. I am like You. As You are in this world, so am I.

You place a mantel of authority on my shoulder and a ring of love on my finger. You crown me with loving kindness.

Together we move; together we reign; together we proclaim, "On earth as it is in Heaven."

Prayers of Prophetic Declaration

-16-

Yours

"Beloved, my lover is mine and I am his..." Songs 2:16

My heart longs after You. I thirst for You like a deer in need of water. My very inner self, the very core of my being cries out to You that I might know You as I am known. My flesh is in need of You. Without Your Presence I am nothing. I love Your face and declare You are my life.

You are the very air I breathe and nothing else can satisfy the longing of my heart other than You. I am the sheep of Your Hand and do not seek or follow another. I hear Your voice and walk accordingly. My heart is captivated by You and I am ravished by Your beauty. I am in the secret place of Your love.

You are my Papa God and I have found You. I have drawn near to You and You have drawn near to me. Your goodness and mercy is passing before me and I am changed.

I am hidden in You under the radar of love. Security and safety is my inheritance within the secret place.

I believe and walk uprightly with a heart of faith. I trust in You and You alone. I have the mind of Christ and contain the thoughts and intents of Your heart.

The eyes of my heart are opened to revelation and understanding for Your light is shining into me separating all darkness. I am a light set on a hill and everyone who looks at me shall see You.

I am salt and light wherever I go and in everything I do. My whole being is setting itself *on heavenly things and the things of this world no longer persuade me.*

Jesus, as You are, I am. The enemy is returning all he has stolen, returning it seven-fold for I am walking in Your abundant life.

I am loved by You. You manifest Yourself to me. Today and every day after, I am Yours and You are mine. Today contains new mercies, new graces, new hope and new revelation. You are doing new things in my life and I perceive it.

-17-

Wisdom

"For the Lord gives wisdom, and from his mouth come knowledge and understanding." Proverbs 2:6

I am after Your own heart and you encourage me to ask for wisdom that I may be filled with knowledge and revelation of You.

I cherish wisdom, highly regarding the instruction of Your Word. I partner with You when I rise up and when I lie down. I am filled with insight and understanding into Your purposes and have discernment in all matters, both natural and spiritual.

I have been made righteous by the shedding of Jesus' Blood and have entered into a covenant of peace. My mouth speaks wisdom and I am alive with great understanding. Wisdom keeps, defends and protects me.

Because I listen to Wisdom's voice and incline my heart to understanding I do not fear or have any dread of evil. Everything I put my hand to prospers and my mouth speaks forth the wisdom of God to men.

I seek You Lord like a hidden treasure and my hope is not disappointed. I hold fast to Your instruction and I do not let go. My feet do not slip for they are on Your rock.

You have already gone before me to prepare a way. My steps are ordered by You this day and every day after. I hear Your voice and obey your leading.

I worship You with reverence, awe, and humble praise. My worshipful sacrifice brings me instruction in Wisdom which I seek more than gold; more than the things of this world.

Wisdom is a skillful teacher. I follow Wisdom and therefore, I am skillful and wise. I am rewarded through Wisdom and my hope shall not be cut off.

I am delivered from my enemies because I walk in Godly wisdom. I please You in all I do, allowing knowledge and joy to be my portion. According to The Father, I am the righteousness of Christ Jesus and exemplify Him in prudence, humility, and tender-hearted mercy to all men.

I asked to be filled with wisdom therefore, I am filled. Wisdom fills me with the Creative Spirit of God and is manifest in all I think and do. I walk in the way of righteousness and my paths are just for Wisdom directs my footsteps.

-18-

Beautiful

"And how can they preach unless they are sent? As it is written, "How beautiful are the feet of those who bring good news." Romans 10:15

Lord, You are an infinite God without end or beginning. You know me and all I have experienced. Every detail of my life is important and valuable to You. I will not run to and fro comparing myself, working or performing for Your attention.

Time has no power to stop or hold back anything You desire for me. I will not limit myself by what I see or be disobedient in any way. I step over the boundaries of time which

73

attempts to cloak the true nature of who I am. I am an eternal child of the Most High God, adored and adorned.

Instead of being one who is halted or holds back, I hear the Father's voice and act as Christ did when on the earth. As a result, I am free and others are free as well. In doing this, I have set my eyes beyond the natural to the supernatural where all things are possible.

I am saturated with supernatural prophetic perspective and the Heavenly power of transformation. I am saturated with the power of God to bring about prophetic creativity. I am eternal and not temporal and so I think in eternal ways when it comes to life and actions. I am not cloaked in time. I am cloaked in supernatural, eternal Glory as a living, manifest representation of Christ on the earth.

All the Words You have ever spoken over me have been in Your heart before all time and now are being revealed through the present age and the ages to come. Not one will fall to the ground or come back to You without accomplishing the purpose for which they were sent.

I declare myself to be a keeper of every Word You have given and none will fall into uninhabited places. Your every Word falls into the good soil of my heart to bring forth eternal purposes in supernatural ways.

I declare the desires of the Lord for my life shall unfold step by step as His light fills my path and gives me direction. The thoughts of the Lord's heart for me are available and accessible at all times and I am one who puts my ear to His heart that I might know them. Every Word proceeding from Him has the power to reconcile my heart to His. I choose to embrace each Word with faith.

Those I love and those sent to me, can and will, be changed by the release of an eternal redemptive Word from the Lord. As a result, all generations will be transformed into the beauty He created.

The Lord has consecrated me and set me apart for His good pleasure, not according to my works but according to the redemptive work of the Cross. Therefore, the grace, mercy and call of Papa God on my life will have its way as I surrender my heart. Blessings will flow down through the ages in many profitable and redeeming ways. You make all things beautiful.

I am chosen and I will walk with eternal perspective displaying the beauty and glory of the Lord. Your great unconditional love sets my heart on a course to live outside the limits and confines of time with realization of eternal results. I live in the goodness, mercy, grace, love and hope of Papa God at all times. I live and move within the beating of the Lord's heart to accomplish His will on a moment by moment basis.

The plans and desires of the Lord's heart for me are too numerous to be counted and it will take all of eternity to fulfill them in any measure. His thoughts toward me are more than every grain of sand and the sands of time cannot displace one thought or one plan, for I am with Him far above all things natural. The temporal things of my life are giving way and will give way to the eternal things of His Word and His heart.

I am created in the image of The Father. I am seated far above the tediousness of life and I embrace my position with a fully surrendered heart. I am receiving revelation, truth, wisdom and understanding for the moment and for the ages to come.

I move to the rhythm of Your heart. Your fragrance is the only thing I emanate.

Lord, You loved me for all time and called me beautiful. You looked at me and called me good. My life is being transformed into the reality of Your likeness.

I am a reflection of the beauty of the Lord in every way and in every situation. My heart is fully satisfied with the Lord and the fragrance He has placed in me.

The time of mantling has come. The time of crowning has come and no opinions or Words of men can stop it. The Lord is adorning me according to His pleasure and not according to the opinions and ideas of man.

I am truly one who is beautiful now and for all time to come.

-19-

Intimacy

"…the Spirit of truth. The world cannot accept him, because it neither sees him nor knows him. But you know him, for he lives with you and will be in you." John 14:17

Lord, I am a diligent worker, a passionate worshiper, a forgiving lover of men, a faithful friend.

Your Word is hidden in my heart and produces fruit on a daily basis. Because Your Word is stored in my heart I do no sin against You or any man. I am not easily offended because I love You.

79

You create an intimate place where we can share our hearts, a place of relationship and confidence where we can express the truest language of all-- the mutual expression of devoted love.

I need You more than the air I breathe. I live on every Word proceeding from Your mouth. You are my daily bread. Because I am hidden in You I walk in faith.

Doubt and unbelief have no place in me. I adorn myself with the Spirit of Truth, girding my loins, my place of strength and power with ever-lasting truth.

I dwell in the secret place of Your Presence. I delight in Your love. My ears hear Your heart and my eyes behold Your beauty. I mount upon wings as the eagle and arise to meet with You. You cover me with Your feathers and make me to lie down in rest.

The tabernacle of Your Presence feeds my soul and I am filled. My cup runs over and I rejoice in You.

-20-

Light

"I have come into the world as a light, so that no one who believes in me should stay in darkness." John 12:46

My heart is Your home and Your abiding place. Everything I have been and everything I will ever be is known by You. My past, present and future are precious to You. Not one moment of my life has gone unnoticed by You. Everything I need to do, know or be is in You. All my hope rests peacefully in You, Lord.

I am no longer of this world but I am a new creation. I have been redeemed from the curse and my past has been forgiven.

81

Lord, I press on toward my high calling and do not give ear or attention to the lies of my enemies. My ears are open to the voice of the Lord and the eyes of my heart are being opened moment by moment that I might know Him in the fullness of His resurrection.

My present is a place of abiding in Him and is alive and filled with His Presence. My future is abounding with hope and expectation for I walk by faith and not by sight. The Presence of the Holy Spirit in me is performing all it is meant to do and I am seeing and will see in a whole new way. I found You and now I am a new, beautiful expression of You.

Everything I can do or ever be is contained within the glorious Presence of the Lord in me, the light of His glory. The thoughts and intents of His heart speak to me and show me His desires and purpose for my life. He withholds nothing from me for I am one who walks uprightly.

Destiny and purpose are in me because He is in me and I am in Him. His light is changing me from glory to glory. I am made new.

Lord, Your Word says the Holy Spirit will bring to remembrance all things when they are needed.
I will be verbal and not shrink back. I will dare to say what You say no matter if my situation says otherwise. I will not hide Your light in me.

Your Presence arises in me like a lighthouse. I do not have poverty of spirit, for I am rich in the Lord and have the mind of Christ. The spiritual bank account given to me is full. I choose to make a withdrawal right now. I withdraw from all that has been given to me and I deposit the riches in my spirit to create agreement with the Lord.

Your Presence explodes in me until I am an expressed example and demonstration of Your grace, mercy, love and power. I reflect Your light and reveal Your Presence.

I agree with You which makes the process of walking out my destiny easier and quicker. Your framed the worlds with Your Words and made all things out of that which was invisible. I speak the Words You have given me. Your Glory in me is both illuminated and reflected. I will not base my diligence on how I feel or what I see. I will simply trust in You and believe Your Words are my Words.

I break agreement with words of judgment from others. I rest in the knowledge of who You are in me and I in You. I delight Your Word even it if brings correction.

Lord, You are the redeemer of all things. You are the light of my present life and the one to come. In You there is neither darkness nor shadow of turning. Steadfastness and goodness light my path. I am secure in You and the promises You have made in Your Word. Therefore, I will choose to keep a guard over my lips that they might speak only kindness. I only want to eat the fruit of life born out of righteous and upright speech.

The Words of my mouth and the meditation of my heart are acceptable in Your sight. I rejoice in Your restorative work in my life as I experience Your ever-present love and brilliance each and every moment. I anticipate my future with great delight for the Spirit of the Lord is upon me to share the good news.

Because You are in me, I am a light in this world and I let my light shine to glorify Your name.

-21-

Breath

"This is what God the Lord says-- he who created the heavens and stretched them out, who spread out the earth and all that comes out of it, who gives breath to its people, and life to those who walk on it..." Isaiah 42:5

All You created was good. I am made in Your image and I am a partaker of Your breath into creation. You breathed Your life into me.

Your revelation sets me free. You know me to the very core of my being and love me. You not only know all about me and the things I need now, but all I will need forever! I am awed by the revelation of Your all consuming, never

87

changing, limitless love, unfolding before my eyes. My steps are surely ordered by You.

I relax and rest in Your Presence, never needing to be anxious about anything. You truly know the end from the beginning and I can rest in the assurance of Your love as You cover me all the days of my life. I have all of eternity to share my heart just as You share Yours with me. You breathe on me in the cool of my day with Your fresh fragrant breath.

Eternity begins right now. I move from the past into the moment where all things are possible and make a choice to always agree with You.

I willingly line up with Your Heavenly invasion into my purpose and destiny. I am chosen by You, infused with You, and filled with Your Presence for all eternity. My mind cannot comprehend it all, yet I walk with increasing capacity to apprehend the hope of my calling. I am being filled with your every breath just as Your train filled the temple.

I am a new creation in Christ Jesus. I can depend on You regardless of the times or seasons. The wind and waters of Your Presence flow over the fleshly places of my heart and shift me into agreement with You.

You deposit rich treasures from the depths of Your heart into mine. I come boldly to the Throne of Grace where I am free, unhindered and unashamed because the breath of God has given me life through the precious Blood of the Cross.

I hear You and I am responding with a heart of praise and declaration, I am here.

I receive Your resurrection power. I receive Your grace. I am here.

You enable me to walk on the waters of my life in the power of Your name as I set my face on You. Winds obey the sound of Your voice as You speak peace over my life.

I am a vessel You have chosen to use for Your Glory. I am the love of Your life. I am Your most favorite one. You are pleased with me and I bring a smile to Your face as You set Your gaze upon me.

I breathe every breath in alignment with You.

I receive strength as I breathe your fragrance. I inhale Your richness. I am full and I am satisfied.

-22-

Inheritance

"I pray also that the eyes of your heart may be enlightened in order that you may know the hope to which he has called you, the riches of his glorious inheritance in the saints..."
Eph 1:18

I am complete in Him who is the head of all principality and power (Colossians 2:10).

I am alive with Christ (Ephesians 2:5).

I am free from the law of sin and death (Romans 8:2).

I am far from oppression, and fear does not come near me (Isaiah 54:14).

I am born of God, and the evil one does not touch me (I John 5:18).

I am holy and without blame before Him in love (I Peter 1:16; Ephesians 1:4).

I have the Greater One living in me; greater is He Who is in me than he who is in the world (I John 4:4).

I have the mind of Christ (Philippians 2:5; I Corinthians 2:16).

I have received the gift of righteousness and reign as a king in life by Jesus Christ (Romans 5:17).

I have no lack for my God supplies all of my need according to His riches in glory by Christ Jesus (Philippians 4:19).

I have received the spirit of wisdom and revelation in the knowledge of Jesus, the eyes of my understanding being enlightened (Ephesians 1:17,18).

I am God's child for I am born again of the incorruptible seed of the Word of God, which lives and abides forever (I Peter 1:23).

I have received the power of the Holy Spirit to lay hands on the sick and see them recover, to cast out demons, to speak with new tongues. I have power over all the power of the enemy, and nothing shall by any means harm me (Mark 16:17,18; Luke 10:17,19).

I have put off the old man and have put on the new man, which is renewed in the knowledge after the image of Him Who created me (Colossians 3:9,10).

I have the peace of God that passes all understanding (Philippians 4:7) I have given, and it is given to me; good measure, pressed down, shaken together, and running over, men give into my bosom (Luke 6:38).

I can quench all the fiery darts of the wicked one with my shield of faith (Ephesians 6:16).

I can do all things through Christ Jesus (Philippians 4:13).

I shall do even greater works than Christ Jesus (John 14:12).

I show forth the praises of God Who has called me out of darkness into His marvelous light (I Peter 2:9).

I am God's workmanship, created in Christ unto good works (Ephesians 2:10).

I am a new creature in Christ (II Corinthians 5:17).

I am a spirit being alive to God (I Thessalonians 5:23; Romans 6:11).

I am a believer, and the light of the Gospel shines in my mind (II Corinthians 4:4).

I am a doer of the Word and blessed in my actions (James 1:22,25).

I am the light of the world (Matthew 5:14).

I am a joint-heir with Christ (Romans 8:17).

I am an overcomer by the blood of the Lamb and the word of my testimony (Revelation 12:11).

I am more than a conqueror through Him Who loves me (Romans 8:37).

I am a partaker of His divine nature (II Peter 1:3,4).

I am an ambassador for Christ (II Corinthians 5:20).

I am part of a chosen generation, a royal priesthood, a holy nation, a purchased people (I Peter 2:9).

I am the righteousness of God in Jesus Christ (II Corinthians 5:21).

I am the temple of the Holy Spirit; I am not my own (I Corinthians 6:19).

I am the head and not the tail; I am above only and not beneath (Deuteronomy 28:13).

I am His elect, full of mercy, kindness, humility, and longsuffering (Romans 8:33; Colossians 3:12).

I am forgiven of all my sins and washed in the Blood (Ephesians 1:7).

I am delivered from the power of darkness and translated into God's kingdom (Colossians 1:13).

I am redeemed from the curse of sin, sickness, and poverty (Galatians 3:13; Deuteronomy 28:15-68).

I am firmly rooted, built up, established in my faith and overflowing with gratitude (Colossians 2:7).

I am called of God to be the voice of His praise (II Timothy 1:9; Psalm 66:8).

I am healed by the stripes of Jesus (I Peter 2:24; Isaiah 53:5).

I am strengthened with all might according to His glorious power (Colossians 1:11).

I am raised up with Christ and seated in heavenly places (Colossians 2:12; Ephesians 2:6).

I am greatly loved by God (Colossians 3:12; Romans 1:7; I Thessalonians 1:4; Ephesians 2:4).

I am submitted to God, and the devil flees from me because I resist him in the Name of Jesus (James 4:7).

It is not I who live, but Christ lives in me (Galatians 2:20).

I press on toward the goal to win the prize to which God in Christ Jesus is calling us upward (Philippians 3:14).

For God has not given us a spirit of fear; but of power, love, and a sound mind (II Timothy 1:7).

*It is for freedom He has set me free
(Galatians5:1).*

**If you have a testimony as a result
of partnering with
Prayers of Prophetic Declaration,
Yvonne would like to hear
from you.**

About the Author

Yvonne Martinez

With 25 years experience in prophetic pastoring, emotional healing and trauma resolution, Yvonne serves as co-leader and Pastoral Counseling staff in the Transformation Center at Bethel Church in Redding, CA.

Yvonne holds a CADCII drug and alcohol credential and is the educational director for CARE-EDU, offering approved drug and alcohol education toward certification. Visit www.care-edu.com

As an ordained minister, Yvonne's passion is to see people acquire their Kingdom identity, inheritance, intimacy and authority. She is available for speaking or personal ministry and the author of 12 books.

www.yvonnem.org

www.care-edu.com

Contact Information

Yvonne Martinez

(530) 229-7909 x 3040

yvonnem@ibethel.org

Bethel Church	www.ibethel.org
Sozo Ministry	www.bethelsozo.com

Books available at

www.yvonnem.org

Made in the USA
San Bernardino, CA
21 May 2020

72107433R00058